Experiencing Chinese

国际语言研究与发展中心

体验汉语®

练习册
高中

Workbook
High School

1A

M000295437

高等教育出版社
Higher Education Press

Contents　目录

Have a try 试一试

① **Look at the pictures and make conversations with your partner.**
看图说话

例：你好。我叫_____。
_____，你好。

玛丽

② **Put the jigsaw pieces in the right position.**
选择正确位置

你 ， 我 C 玛丽 D 。

③ **On your own.**
活动

Passing down 击鼓传花

One student hits the drum while the others pass down the "flower". If you get the "flower" when the drumbeat stops, you should say hello and introduce yourself to the class. Continue the game after you are done.

鼓响时学生们开始传花，鼓声停止时，持花者向大家问好，并介绍自己。完毕后，接着进行下一次击鼓传花游戏。

例：你好，我叫_____。

Practice and learn 练一练

一 *Pinyin* exercises
拼音练习

① **Listen to the CD and repeat.**
听录音，并跟读下列音节

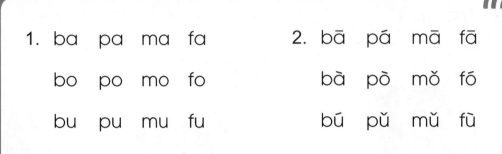

1. ba pa ma fa   2. bā pá mā fā

bo po mo fo   bà pò mǒ fó

bu pu mu fu   bú pǔ mǔ fū

② **Listen to the CD and then fill in the initials or the finals.**
听录音，填写声母或韵母

• **Please fill in the initials.**
请填写声母

__ěi   __ì   __ò
__ǎo   __iǎo   __áng
__ái   __ó
__én   __éng

• **Please fill in the finals.**
请填写韵母

w__ l__ n__ b__
h__ d__ n__ f__
t__ m__

③ **Listen to the CD and then mark the tones.**
听录音，标出声调

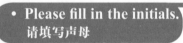

1. wo   2. ke   3. yi   4. ba   5. xi

6. ni   7. qu   8. chi   9. xie   10. wan

④ **Listen to the CD and then circle the syllables you've heard.**
听录音，在听到的拼音上画圈

❶	bù	pù	❻	bǎn	pàn
❷	bǐ	pǐ	❼	bīn	pīn
❸	bà	pà	❽	biě	piě
❹	bó	pó	❾	běng	pěng
❺	bèi	pèi	❿	biàn	piàn

二 **Word exercises**
词汇练习
① **Matching.**
连线

你 好
我
叫
早

晚
他
上 下 们

wǒ
jiào
nǐ
hǎo
shàng
men
xiǎ
wǎn
tā
zǎo

② **Crossword puzzles.**
填字游戏

● **Put the following words in the blanks.**
请把下列汉字填在田字格里。

叫 早 我 晚 你

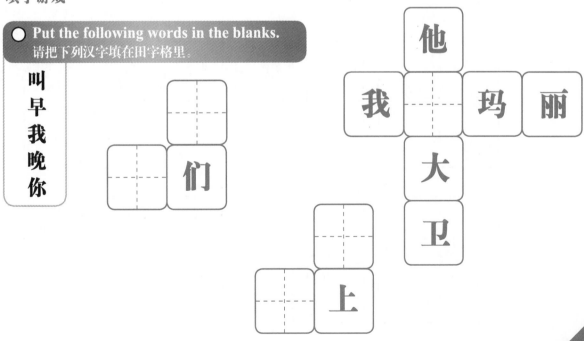

他

我　　玛 丽

大

卫

们

上

三 Chinese character exercises
汉字练习

① Learn to recognize.
　认汉字

○ Count the strokes of the following characters, and then compare your answers with your partner's.
数一数下列每个汉字有多少笔画，并与同伴比较一下，看谁数得对。

你 ○	好 ○	我 ○	叫 ○	早 ○

② Learn to divide.
　拆汉字

早 ➤ 日 + 十　　　他 ➤ ○ + ○

晚 ➤ ○ + ○　　　好 ➤ ○ + ○

们 ➤ ○ + ○　　　叫 ➤ ○ + ○

你 ➤ ○ + ○

③ Learn to write.
　写汉字

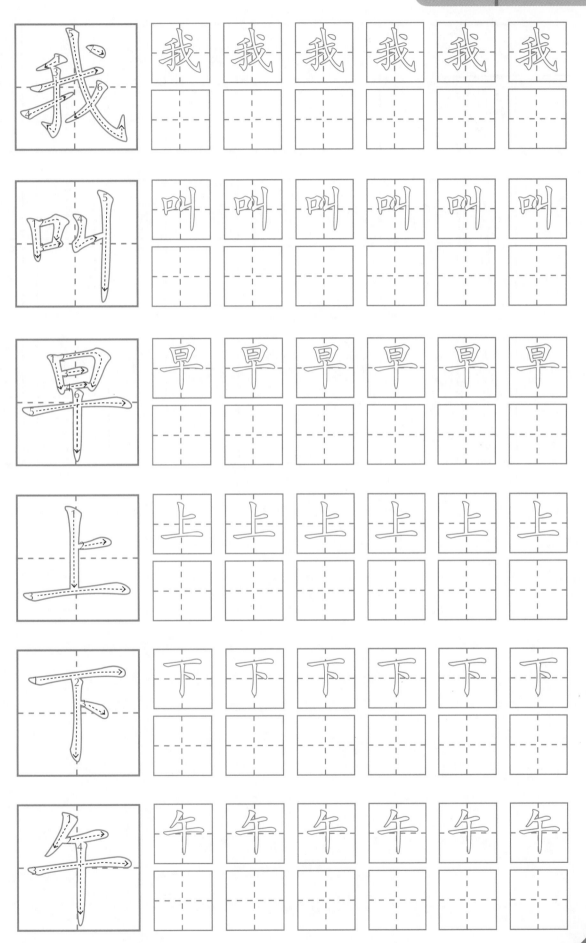

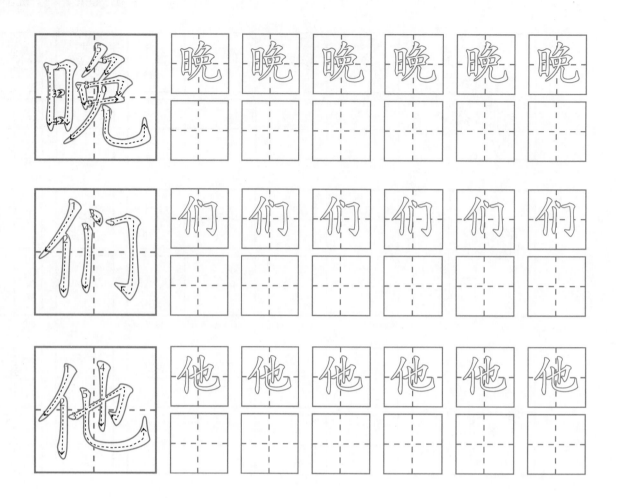

晚 晚 晚 晚 晚 晚

们 们 们 们 们 们

他 他 他 他 他 他

Have a try 试一试

① **Look at the pictures and make conversations with your partner.**
看图说话

例：＿＿＿＿＿叫什么名字？
＿＿＿＿＿叫＿＿＿＿＿。

成龙

妹妹 玛丽

老师 珍妮

弟弟 迈克

② **Put the jigsaw piece in the right position.**
选择正确位置

A：老师，您 姓？

B：我 姓王，你 姓什么？

 贵

A：我 姓马。

③ **On your own.**
活动

Making a name tag 做名签

Make a pretty, unique name tag about yourself, including your English name, Chinese name and *Pinyin*.

为自己制作一个美观漂亮、有个性的名签，内容包括：英文名字、中文名字和汉语拼音。

Mary
Mǎlì
玛丽

Practice and learn 练一练

一 *Pinyin* exercises
拼音练习

① **Listen to the CD and repeat.**
听录音，并跟读下列音节

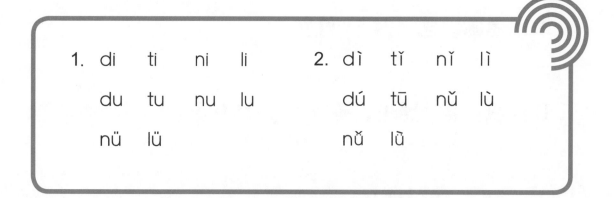

1.	di	ti	ni	li	2.	dì	tǐ	nǐ	lì
	du	tu	nu	lu		dú	tū	nǔ	lù
	nü	lü				nǔ	lǚ		

2 Listen to the CD and then fill in the initials or the finals.
听录音，填写声母或韵母

• **Please fill in the initials.**
请填写声母

__ é   __ óng   __ à

__ āng   __ ái   __ ōu

__ ài   __ ín

__ ǎo   __ à

• **Please fill in the finals.**
请填写韵母

l __   zh __   q __

d __   n __   x __

b __   l __   ch __

j __

3 Listen to the CD and then mark the tones.
听录音，标出声调

1. di   2. xing   3. ming   4. nin   5. wu

6. nü   7. lü   8. gui   9. zhuo   10. peng

4 Listen to the CD and then circle the syllables you've heard.
听录音，在听到的拼音上画圈

1	dì	tì	6	duō	tuō
2	dù	tù	7	dào	tào
3	dà	tà	8	dīng	tīng
4	dài	tài	9	diān	tiān
5	diē	tiē	10	dǒng	tǒng

二 Word exercises
词汇练习
① Matching.
连线

② Crossword puzzles.
填字游戏

● **Put the following words in the blanks.**
请把下列汉字填在田字格里。

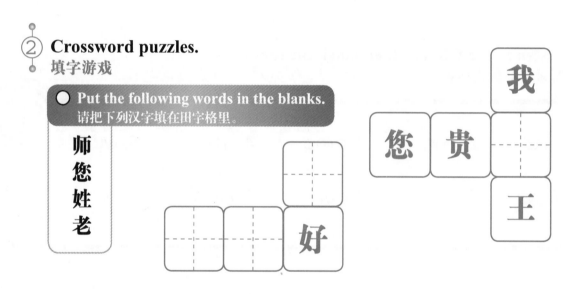

师 您 姓 老

三 Chinese character exercises
汉字练习
① Learn to recognize.
认汉字

● Count the strokes of the following characters, and then compare your answers with your partner's.
数一数下列每个汉字有多少笔画，并与同伴比较一下，看谁数得对。

姓 什 么 名 师

② **Learn to divide.**
拆汉字

什 ➤ ⑴ + ⑴   您 ➤ ◯ + ◯

姓 ➤ ◯ + ◯   妹 ➤ ◯ + ◯

她 ➤ ◯ + ◯   字 ➤ ◯ + ◯

③ **Learn to write.**
写汉字

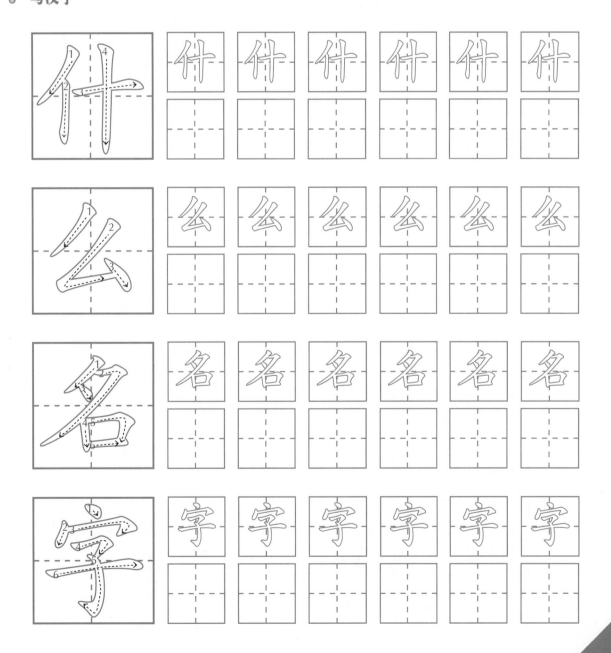

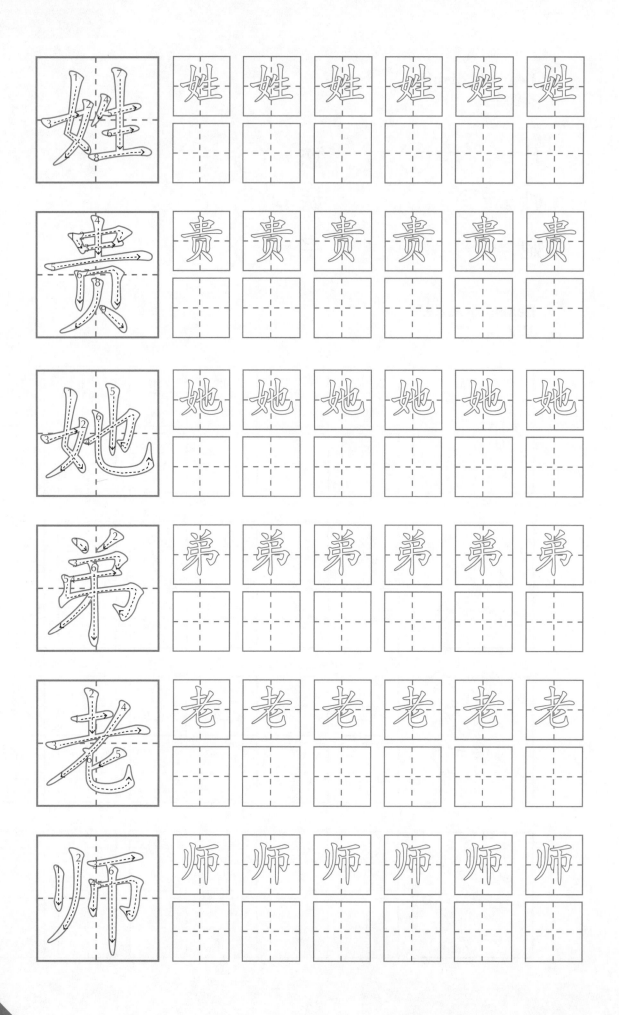

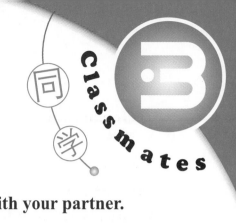
Have a try 试一试

① **Look at the pictures and make conversations with your partner.**
看图说话

例： 他/她是谁?
他/她是_____的_____。

妹妹 朋友

妈妈 学生

弟弟 老师

我 同学

② **Put the jigsaw pieces in the right position.**
选择正确位置

的

1. 我们 A 是 B 他 C 学生 D 。

新

2. 我 A 是 B 你们 C 的 D 老师。

3. 王阿姨 A 是 B 妈妈 C 的 D
朋友。

好

③ On your own.
活动

Introduction 人物介绍

Bring a photo of your friends, classmates or family members to class. Introduce them to your classmates following the examples below.

准备一张朋友、同学或家人的照片，仿照例子，向大家介绍一下。

例：他/她是我的好朋友/小学同学/弟弟，
    他（她）叫＿＿＿＿＿＿。

Practice and learn 练一练

一 *Pinyin* exercises
拼音练习

① Listen to the CD and repeat.
听录音，并跟读下列音节

1.	gai	kai	hai		2.	gāi	kǎi	hái
	gei	kei	hei			gěi	kēi	hēi
	gui	kui	hui			guì	kuì	huì

② Listen to the CD and then fill in the initials or the finals.
听录音，填写声母或韵母

• Please fill in the initials. 请填写声母
＿＿ òu ＿＿ āi ＿＿ uì
＿＿ ǎo ＿＿ àn ＿＿ ǒng
＿＿ āo ＿＿ uí
＿＿ àn ＿＿ ǎo

• Please fill in the finals. 请填写韵母
b ＿＿ h ＿＿ z ＿＿
s ＿＿ f ＿＿ n ＿＿
b ＿＿ h ＿＿
m ＿＿ d ＿＿

③ **Listen to the CD and then mark the tones.**
听录音，标出声调

1. ge	2. ku	3. hai	4. hen	5. jia
6. tong	7. xue	8. you	9. xiao	10. huan

④ **Listen to the CD and then circle the syllables you've heard.**
听录音，在听到的拼音上画圈

①	gē	kē	⑥	guǒ	kuǒ
②	gàn	kàn	⑦	guà	kuà
③	gū	kū	⑧	gào	kào
④	gǒu	kǒu	⑨	gēng	kēng
⑤	gāi	kāi	⑩	gōng	kōng

二 Word exercises
词汇练习
① **Matching.**
连线

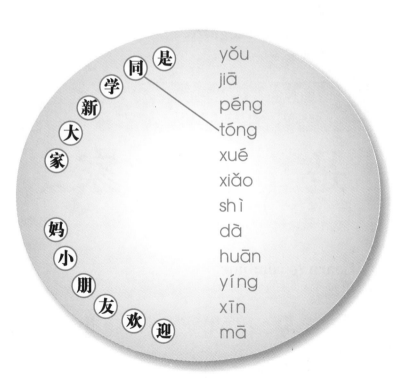

② **Crossword puzzles.**
填字游戏

● **Put the following words in the blanks.**
请把下列汉字填在田字格里。

大 同 学 妈 友 小 家 同 妈 朋

新

学

好

三 **Chinese character exercises**
汉字练习
① **Learn to recognize.**
认汉字

● **Count the strokes of the following characters, and then compare your answers with your partner's.**
数一数下列每个汉字有多少笔画，并与同伴比较一下，看谁数得对。

是 ○　同 ○　家 ○　学 ○　友 ○

② **Learn to combine.**
组汉字

白 + 勺 ➤ 的　　　月 + 月 ➤ ○

亲 + 斤 ➤ ○　　　又 + 欠 ➤ ○

阝 + 可 ➤ ◯　　　辶 + 卬 ➤ ◯

⺌ + 子 ➤ ◯　　　女 + 马 ➤ ◯

③ **Learn to write.**
写汉字

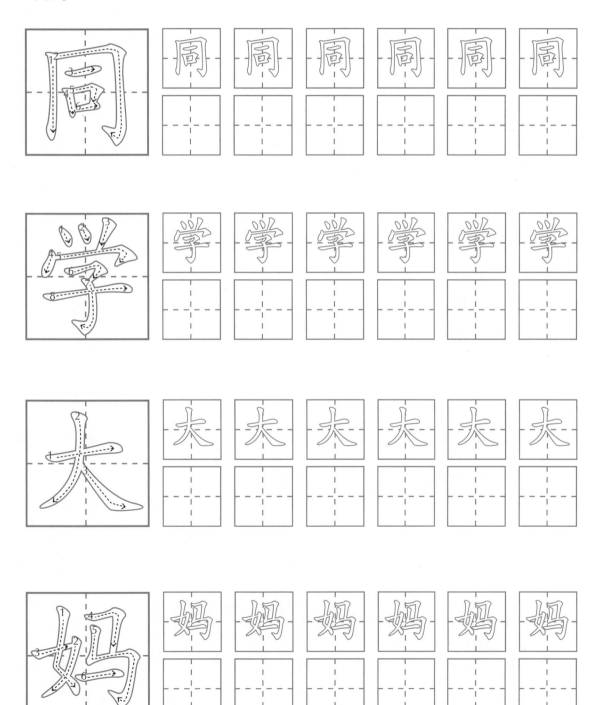

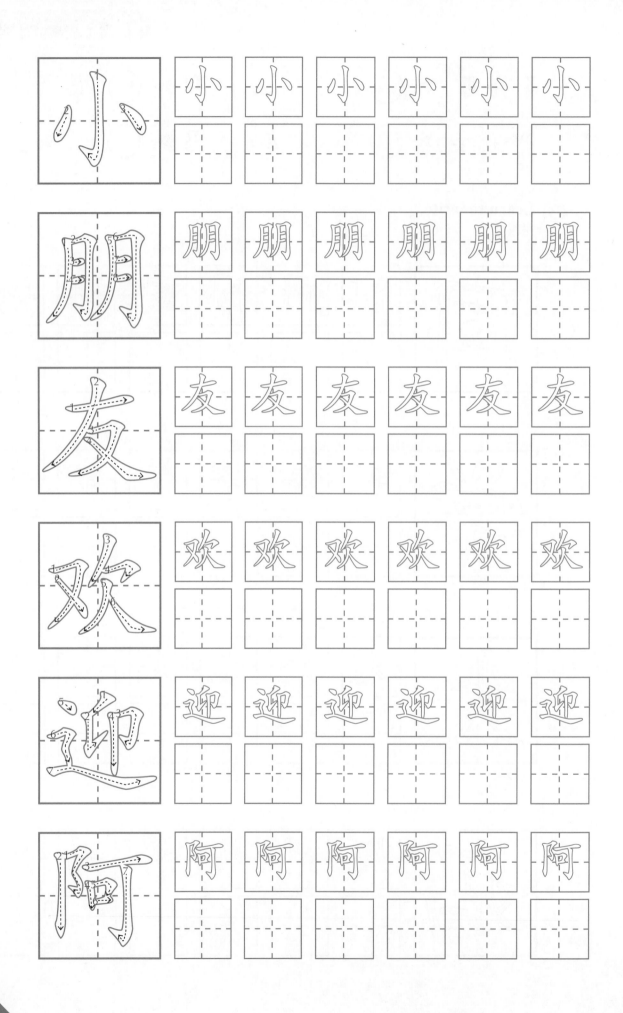

小　小　小　小　小　小

朋　朋　朋　朋　朋　朋

友　友　友　友　友　友

欢　欢　欢　欢　欢　欢

迎　迎　迎　迎　迎　迎

阿　阿　阿　阿　阿　阿

Have a try 试一试

① Look at the pictures and make conversations with your partner.
看图说话

例：1. 这是＿＿＿＿＿＿，那是＿＿＿＿＿＿。
2. 这些是＿＿＿＿＿＿，那些是＿＿＿＿＿＿。

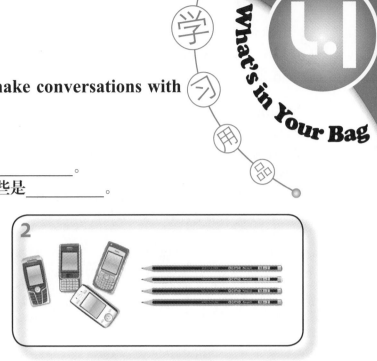

② Put the jigsaw pieces in the right position.
选择正确位置

1. 这 A 是 B 汉语 C 书 D ？ 吗

2. 这 AC 是 B 汉语书，这是 C 汉语 D 字典。 不

3. 玛丽 A 是我的小学同学，B 王明 C 是我的 D 小学同学。 也

③ On your own.
活动

Passing down 击鼓传花

One student hits the drum while the others pass down the "flower". If you get the "flower", you should talk about your or others' stationery. Continue the game after you are done.

鼓响时学生们开始传花，鼓声停止时，持花者向大家介绍自己或他人的学习用品。完毕后，接着进行下一次击鼓传花游戏。

例：这是 _____，那是 _____。
这些是 _____，那些是 _____。

Practice and learn 练一练

一 *Pinyin* exercises
拼音练习

① Listen to the CD and repeat.
听录音，并跟读下列音节

1.	ji	qi	xi		2.	jǐ	qì	xī
	ju	qu	xu			jǔ	qù	xū
	jie	qie	xie			jiē	qiè	xié

② Listen to the CD and then fill in the initials.
听录音，填写声母

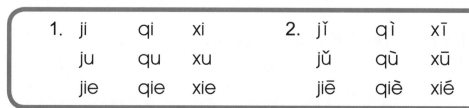

- **Please fill in the initials.**
  请填写声母

___iě	___ǐ	___īn	___iū	___ī	___ián
___ué	___ù	___iā	___ǐng	___iǎo	___iǎng
___iān	___iǔ	___īn	___uǎn	___uè	___iǎn
___iǎo	___iǎ				

③ **Listen to the CD and then mark the tones.**
听录音，标出声调

1. ji	2. qian	3. shou	4. ye	5. dian
6. yu	7. bu	8. shuai	9. ti	10. jia

④ **Listen to the CD and then circle the syllables you've heard.**
听录音，在听到的拼音上画圈

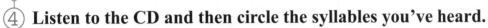

❶	lē	lè		❻	qiān	qiàn
❷	lāo	lào		❼	xiē	xiè
❸	tā	tà		❽	hān	hàn
❹	zhē	zhè		❾	jiā	jià
❺	shōu	shǒu		❿	guī	guì

二 **Word exercises**
词汇练习

① **Matching.**
连线

shǒu
bù
hàn
zhè
shū
nà
yě
bǐ
yǔ
xiē

这 那 手 笔 不 些 书 也 汉 语

② **Crossword puzzles.**
填字游戏

● **Put the following words in the blanks.**
请把下列汉字填在田字格里。

典那手名典机字这

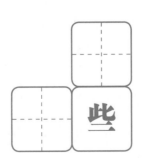

些

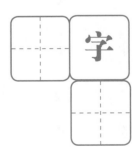

字

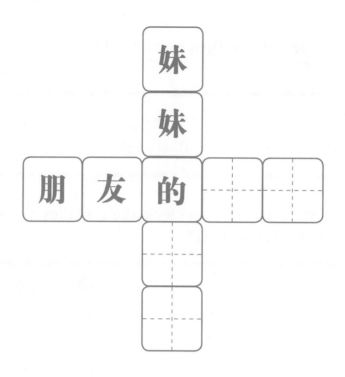

三 **Chinese character exercises**
汉字练习

① **Learn to recognize.**
认汉字

○ Count the strokes of the following characters, and then compare your answers with your partner's.
数一数下列每个汉字有多少笔画，并与同伴比较一下，看谁数得对。

| 手 ○ | 不 ○ | 书 ○ | 也 ○ | 典 ○ |

② **Learn to combine.**
组汉字

辶 ＋ 文 ➤ 这   竹 ＋ 毛 ➤ ○

木 ＋ 几 ➤ ○   氵 ＋ 又 ➤ ○

口 ＋ 马 ➤ ○   钅 ＋ 슴 ➤ ○

尹 ＋ 阝 ➤ ○   讠 ＋ 吾 ➤ ○

③ **Learn to write.**
写汉字

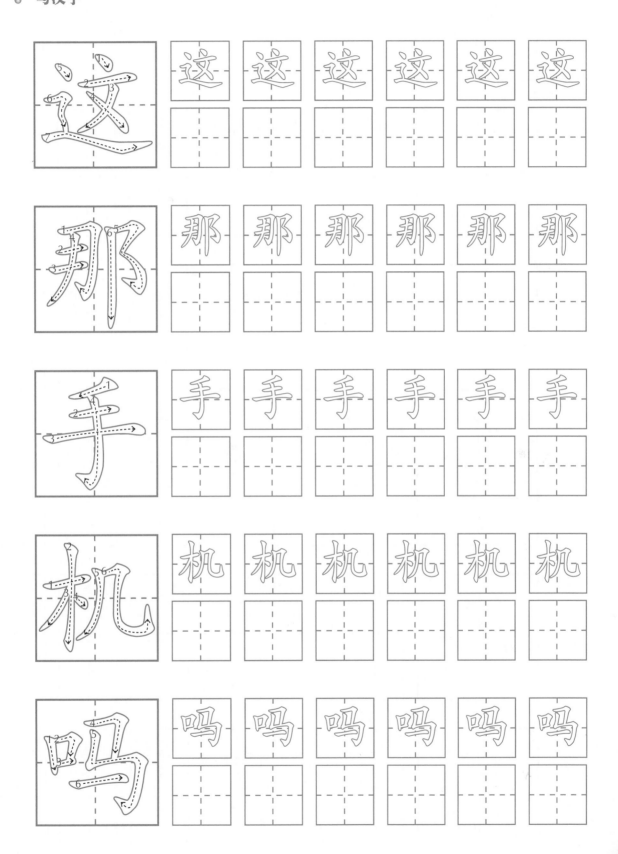

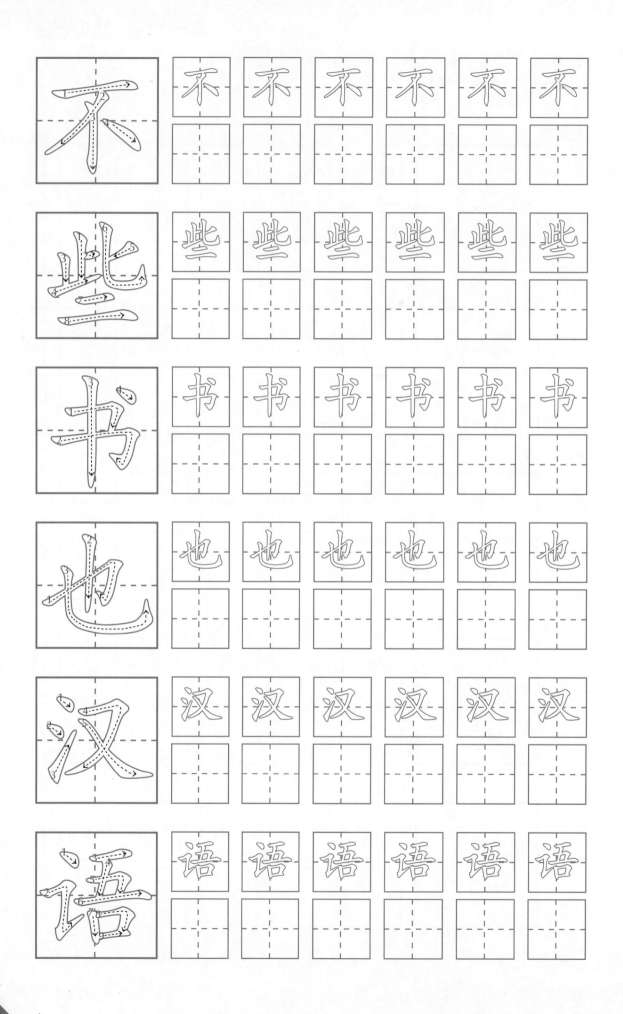

不　不　不　不　不　不

些　些　些　些　些　些

书　书　书　书　书　书

也　也　也　也　也　也

汉　汉　汉　汉　汉　汉

语　语　语　语　语　语

Have a try 试一试

① **Look at the pictures and make conversations with your partner.**
看图说话

例：A：这是谁?
　　B：这是我_____，他（她）是_____（职业 job）。

姐姐　　　　　叔叔　　　　　爸爸　　　　　妈妈

② **Put the jigsaw pieces in the right position.**
选择正确位置

1.

2.

3. A 他　B 爸爸　C 真　D 。

③ On your own.
活动

Introduction 家人介绍

Take a photo of your family to class. Introduce your family members and their professions to your classmates. Follow the examples below.

将一张全家人的照片带到学校，向同学们介绍自己的家人及其职业。

例：这是我爸爸/妈妈/哥哥/姐姐/弟弟/妹妹，他（她）是_____。

Practice and learn 练一练

一 *Pinyin* exercises
拼音练习

① **Listen to the CD and repeat.**
听录音，并跟读下列音节

1. zhi chi shi ri   2. zhāo cháo shǎo rào

    zhe che she re   zhōu chōu shòu ròu

    zhu chu shu ru   jiǔ   qiú   xiū   niú

② **Listen to the CD and then fill in the initials or the finals.**
听录音，填写声母或韵母

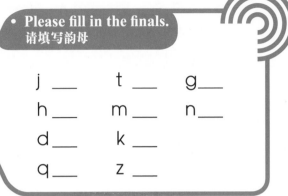

- **Please fill in the initials.**
  请填写声母

  __ē   __à   __uí

  __ēn   __ū   __ǎo

  __ǒu   __én

  __ē   __ǎo

- **Please fill in the finals.**
  请填写韵母

  j __   t __   g__

  h __   m __   n__

  d __   k __

  q__   z __

③ **Listen to the CD and then mark the tones.**
听录音，标出声调

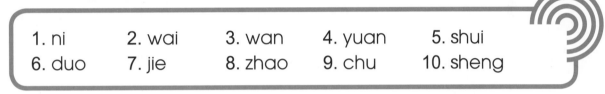

1. ni   2. wai   3. wan   4. yuan   5. shui

6. duo   7. jie   8. zhao   9. chu   10. sheng

④ **Listen to the CD and then circle the syllables you've heard.**
听录音，在听到的拼音上画圈

①	ní	nǐ	⑥	shí	shǐ
②	zāo	zǎo	⑦	guó	guǒ
③	wú	wǔ	⑧	hén	hěn
④	qíng	qǐng	⑨	xiáng	xiǎng
⑤	lāo	lǎo	⑩	quán	quǎn

二 **Word exercises**
词汇练习

① **Matching.**
连线

谁   yī
姐   zhēn
真   shuí
年   gē
轻   jiě
     bà
照   qīng
爸   nián
医   zhào
叔 哥   shū

②**Crossword puzzles.**
填字游戏

◯ **Put the following words in the blanks.**
请把下列汉字填在田字格里。

多 谁 医 哥 学 家 哥

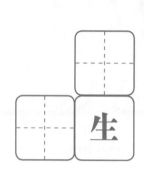

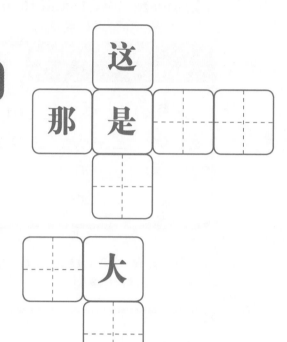

三 **Chinese character exercises**
汉字练习

① **Learn to recognize.**
认汉字

◯ Count the strokes of the following characters, and then compare your answers with your partner's.
数一数下列每个汉字有多少笔画，并与同伴比较一下，看谁数得对。

多 ◯　真 ◯　年 ◯　片 ◯　司 ◯

② **Learn to divide.**
拆汉字

谁 ➤ ⓘ + 隹　　护 ➤ ◯ + ◯

姐 ➤ ◯ + ◯　　叔 ➤ ◯ + ◯

轻 ➤ ◯ + ◯　　医 ➤ ◯ + ◯

爸 ➤ ◯ + ◯　　照 ➤ ◯ + ◯

30

③ **Learn to write.**
写汉字

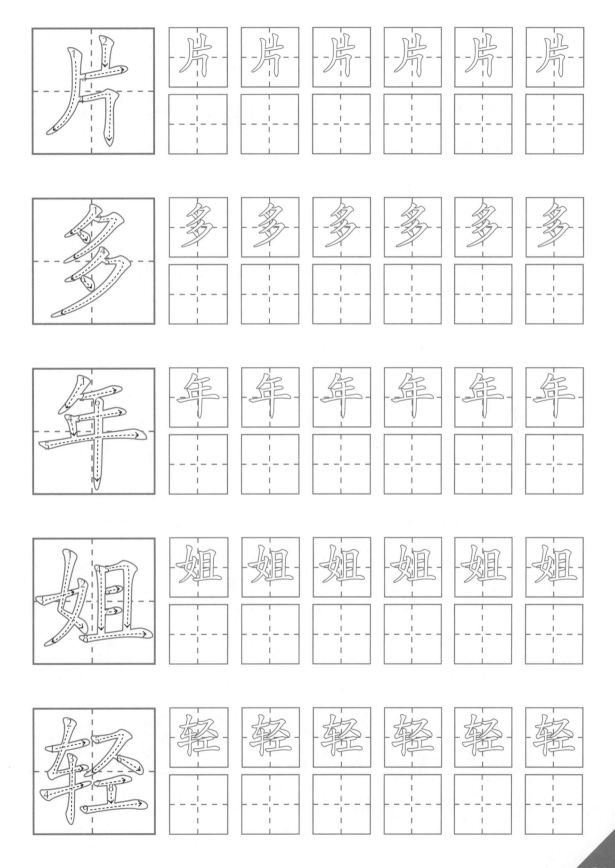

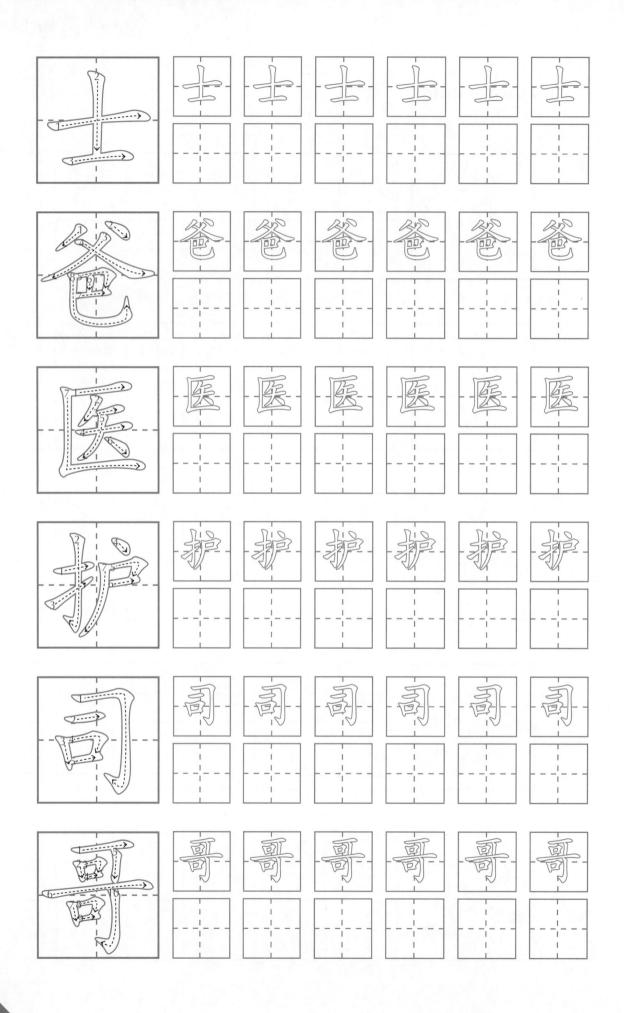

Have a try 试一试

① **Look at the pictures and make conversations with your partner.**
看图说话

例：A：_____在哪儿?
　　B：_____在_____的
　　　上面/下面/左边/右边/旁边。

② **Put the jigsaw pieces in the right position.**
选择正确位置

1. A 玛丽 B 的 C 铅笔 D 哪儿? 在

2. 妈妈 A 的手机 B 在沙发 C 面 D 。 上

3. 妹妹的 A 书包 B 在椅子的 C 面 D 。 下

③ **On your own.**
活动

Making a telephone directory 小制作

Make a telephone directory of your family members, friends and classmates.
调查家人、朋友和同学的电话号码，制作一个电话本。

姓名	电话号码

Practice and learn 练一练

一 *Pinyin* exercises
拼音练习

① **Listen to the CD and repeat.**
听录音，并跟读下列音节

1. zi   ci   si   2. zì   cì   sì
   za   ca   sa   zá   cā   sà
   ze   ce   se   zé   cè   sè
   zu   cu   su   zú   cù   sū

② **Listen to the CD and then fill in the initials.**
听录音，填写声母

- **Please fill in the initials.**
  请填写声母

___ è ___ ān ___ ǎo ___ uī ___ uó ___ ài ___ ǒng

___ ǎo ___ è ___ ā ___ uì ___ uǒ ___ uò

___ ì ___ ài ___ ǐ ___ ān ___ ǒu ___ ōng

③ **Listen to the CD and then mark the tones.**
听录音，标出声调

1. bao 2. fa 3. pang 4. bi 5. zuo
6. chuang 7. yi 8. shi 9. mei 10. liu

④ **Listen to the CD and then circle the syllables you've heard.**
听录音，在听到的拼音上画圈

① zū	zhù	⑥	céng	chéng
② zì	zhì	⑦	sǎo	shǎo
③ zǎo	zhǎo	⑧	sōu	shōu
④ cuī	chuī	⑨	sǎn	shǎng
⑤ cǎn	chǎn	⑩	sè	shè

二 **Word exercises**
词汇练习
① **Matching.**
连线

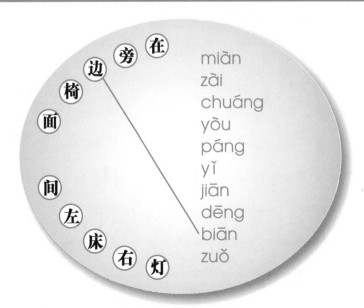

在 旁 边 椅 面 间 左 床 右 灯

miàn
zài
chuáng
yòu
páng
yǐ
jiān
dēng
biān
zuǒ

② **Crossword puzzles.**
填字游戏

> ○ **Put the following words in the blanks.**
> 请把下列汉字填在田字格里。

下
子
右
上
左

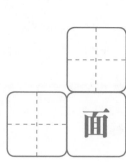

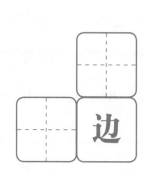

三 **Chinese character exercises**
汉字练习
① **Learn to recognize.**
认汉字

> ○ **Count the strokes of the following characters, and then compare your answers with your partner's.**
> 数一数下列每个汉字有多少笔画，并与同伴比较一下，看谁数得对。

包 ○　在 ○　发 ○　子 ○　左 ○

② **Learn to divide.**
拆汉字

钥 ➤ 钅 + 月　　房 ➤ ○ + ○

沙 ➤ ○ + ○　　间 ➤ ○ + ○

边 ➤ ○ + ○　　床 ➤ ○ + ○

椅 ➤ ○ + ○　　灯 ➤ ○ + ○

③ Learn to write.
写汉字

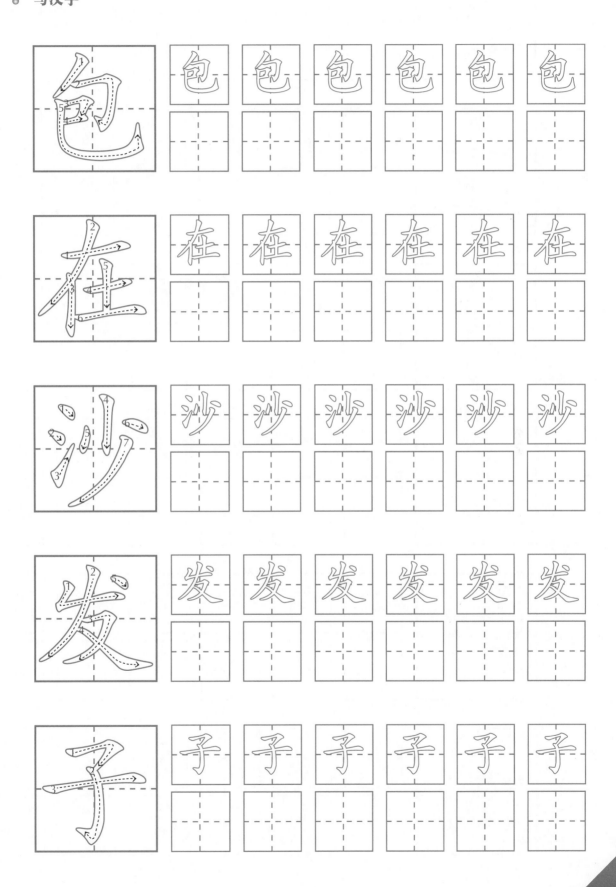

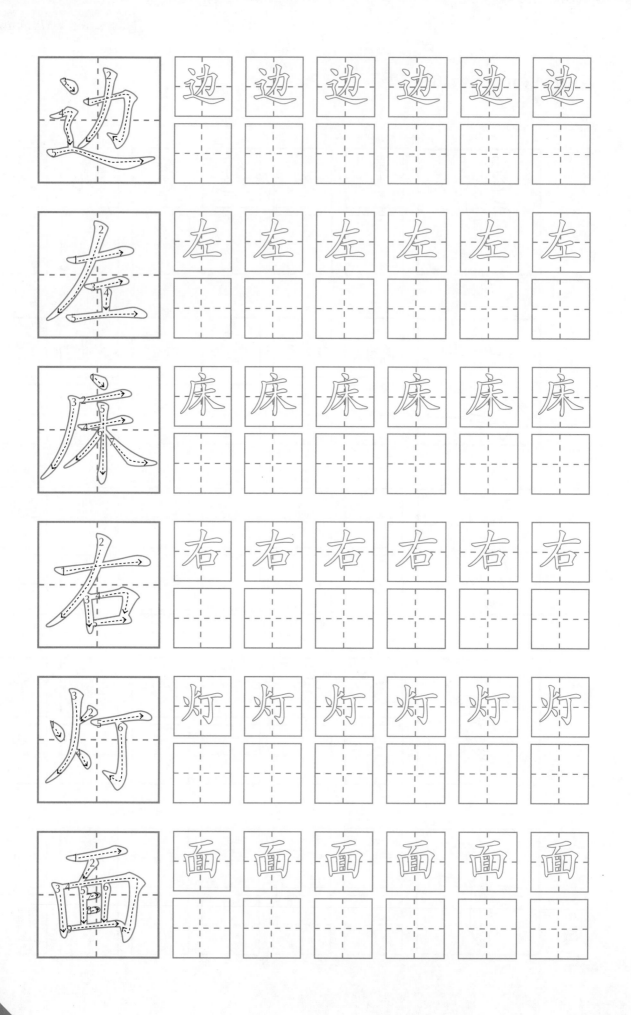

Have a try 试一试

① **Look at the pictures and make conversations with your partner.**
看图说话

Please color the things in the picture, and then practice with your partner.
请将图片里的物品涂上各种颜色，并与同伴练习。

例: _____是什么颜色的?
_____是黄/红/白/黑/绿/蓝/
灰/粉色的。

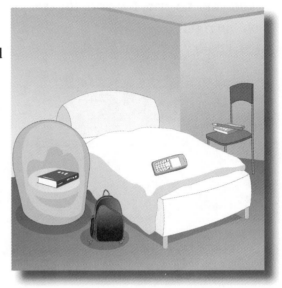

② **Put the jigsaw pieces in the right position.**
选择正确位置

1. **A** 哥哥 **B** 的 **C** 书包在 **D** 。 **这儿**

2. 你的手机 **A** 是 **B** 什么 **C** 颜色 **D** ? **的**

3. **A** 他 **B** 的房间 **C** 真 **D** ! **漂亮**

③ On your own.
活动

Coloring 涂颜色

Add your favorite colors to the two pictures on the right.
将右边的两个人物涂上自己喜欢的颜色。

例：女生： A——粉色　B——蓝色　C——白色
　　　　　D——黑色　E——红色

　　　男生： F——黄色　G——绿色
　　　　　H——黑色　I——灰色

Practice and learn 练一练

一 *Pinyin* exercises
拼音练习

① **Listen to the CD and repeat.**
听录音，并跟读下列音节

1.	nie	nüe		2.	māma	gēge
	lie	lüe			tāde	yéye
	jie	jue			qīzi	jiějie
	qie	que			dìdi	wǒde
	xie	xue			bàba	sǎozi

② **Listen to the CD and then fill in the finals.**
听录音，填写韵母

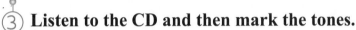
- **Please fill in the finals.**
  请填写韵母

q __   l __   x __   b __   x __   d __

n __   j __   j __   q __   t __   l __

m __   p __   n __

③ **Listen to the CD and then mark the tones.**
听录音，标出声调

1. xue   2. gao   3. qiu   4. pang   5. ku
6. zhou   7. deng   8. ying   9. zuo   10. wang

④ **Listen to the CD and then circle the syllables you've heard.**
听录音，在听到的拼音上画圈

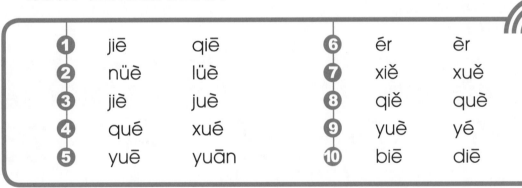

1 jiē qiē   6 ér èr
2 nüè lüè   7 xiě xuě
3 jiè juè   8 qiě què
4 qué xué   9 yuè yé
5 yuē yuān   10 biē diē

二 **Word exercises**
词汇练习
① **Matching.**
连线

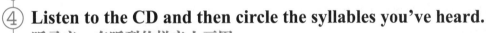

○ **Put the following words in the blanks.**
请把下列汉字填在田字格里。

红 哪 这 黑 年 漂 轻 亮

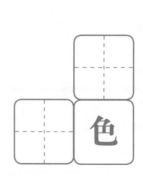

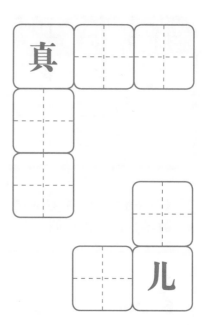

三 **Chinese character exercises**
汉字练习
① **Learn to recognize.**
认汉字

○ **Count the strokes of the following characters, and then compare your answers with your partner's.**
数一数下列每个汉字有多少笔画，并与同伴比较一下，看谁数得对。

色 ○ 黑 ○ 亮 ○ 白 ○ 灰 ○

② **Learn to combine.**
组汉字

 + 文 ➤ 这   纟 + 工 ➤ ○

纟 + 录 ➤ ○   氵 + 票 ➤ ○

彦 + 页 ➤ ○   艹 + 监 ➤ ○

③ **Learn to write.**
写汉字

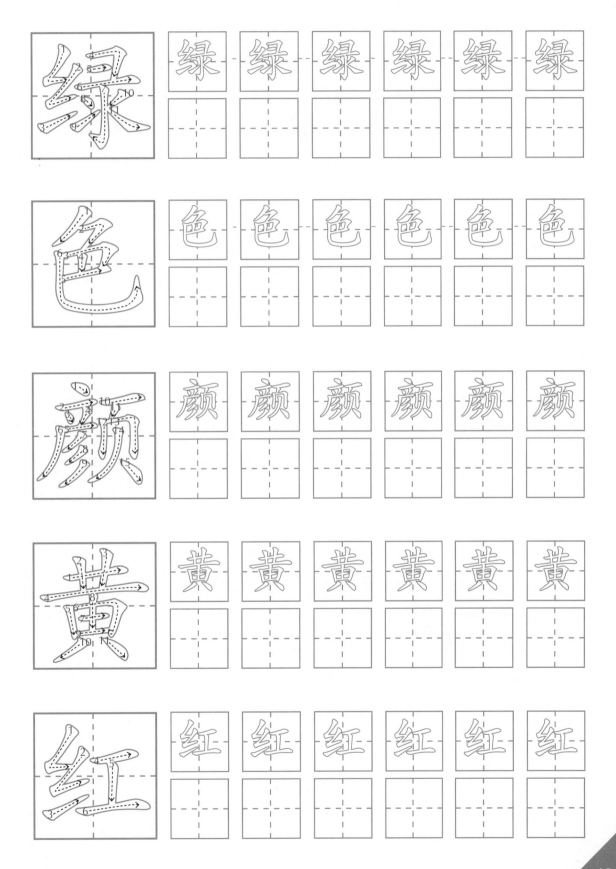

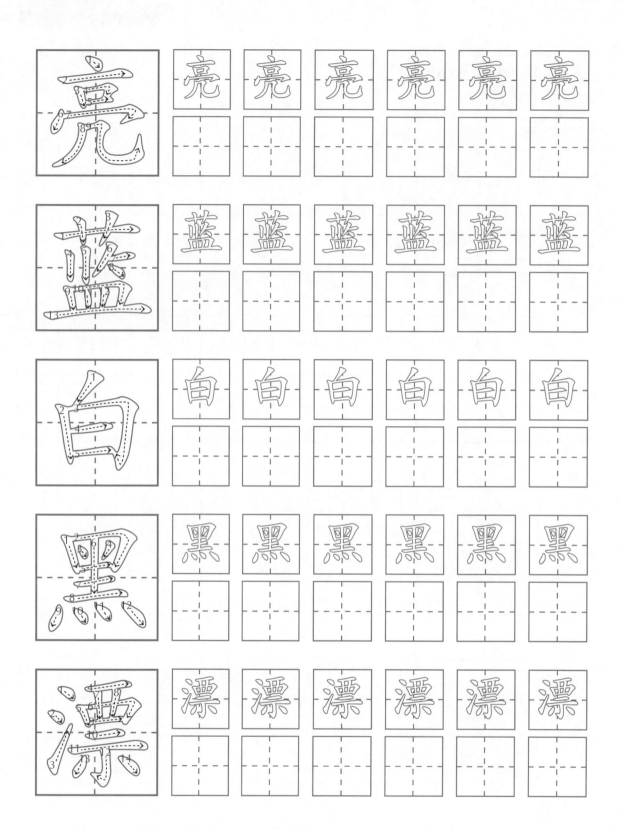

亮　亮　亮　亮　亮　亮

藍　藍　藍　藍　藍　藍

白　白　白　白　白　白

黑　黑　黑　黑　黑　黑

漂　漂　漂　漂　漂　漂

Have a try 试一试

① **Look at the pictures and make conversations with your partner.**

看图说话

例: A: _____ 喜欢什么动物?
　　B: _____ 喜欢 _____。

② **Put the jigsaw pieces in the right position.**

选择正确位置

1. A 你 B 什么 C 动物 D ？　喜欢

2. A 他 B 家 C 有猫 D 。　　没 C

3. 我 A 不 B 喜欢狗 C ，你 D ？　呢

On your own.
活动

Talking about pets 谈宠物

Work in groups. Talk about your favorite animals and their colors. Then complete the following form.

几人一组谈谈自己喜欢的动物及这种动物的颜色，并填写下面的表格。

同学的名字	喜欢的动物	动物的颜色
大卫	狗	黄色

Practice and learn 练一练

一 *Pinyin* exercises
拼音练习

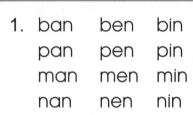 **Listen to the CD and repeat.**
听录音，并跟读下列音节

1. ban   ben   bin
     pan   pen   pin
     man   men   min
     nan   nen   nin

2. bān   bèn   bīn
     pán   mán   fán
     pén   mén   fēn
     pǐn   mín   nín

② **Listen to the CD and then fill in the finals.**
听录音，填写韵母

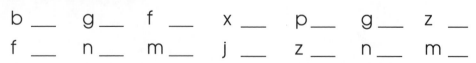 • **Please fill in the finals.**
请填写韵母

b __   g__   f __   x __   p__   g __   z __

f __   n__   m__   j __   z __   n__   m __

k __   h __   d __   q __   r __   m __

③ **Listen to the CD and then mark the tones.**
听录音，标出声调

1. fei	2. ying	3. huang	4. wei	5. bang
6. hao	7. geng	8. yao	9. dou	10. diu

④ **Listen to the CD and then circle the syllables you've heard.**
听录音，在听到的拼音上画圈

① fān	hàn	⑥ zhān	chān
② sān	shān	⑦ mǎn	mǐn
③ hěn	běn	⑧ tán	nán
④ shēn	shēng	⑨ kěn	kǎn
⑤ yín	rén	⑩ lán	láng

二 **Word exercises**
词汇练习
① **Matching.**
连线

对　猫
有
宠
物
喜
狗
它
儿　象

yǒu
gǒu
tā
xiàng
chǒng
jǐ
duì
wǔ
māo
xǐ

② **Crossword puzzles.**
填字游戏

● **Put the following words in the blanks.**
请把下列汉字填在田字格里。

迎
宠
动
喜

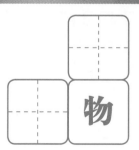

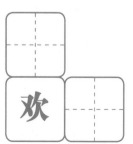

47

三 Chinese character exercises
汉字练习

① Learn to recognize.
认汉字

○ Count the strokes of the following characters, and then compare your answers with your partner's.
数一数下列每个汉字有多少笔画，并与同伴比较一下，看谁数得对。

有 ○　宠 ○　喜 ○　熊 ○　猫 ○

② Learn to combine.
组汉字

犭 + 苗 ➤ 猫　　犭 + 句 ➤ ○

宀 + 龙 ➤ ○　　能 + 灬 ➤ ○

又 + 寸 ➤ ○　　云 + 力 ➤ ○

宀 + 匕 ➤ ○　　氵 + 殳 ➤ ○

牛 + 勿 ➤ ○　　口 + 尼 ➤ ○

③ Learn to write.
写汉字

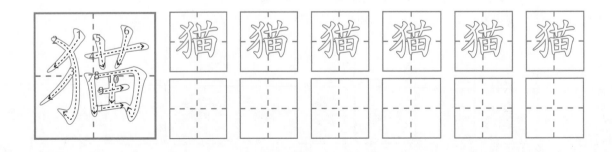

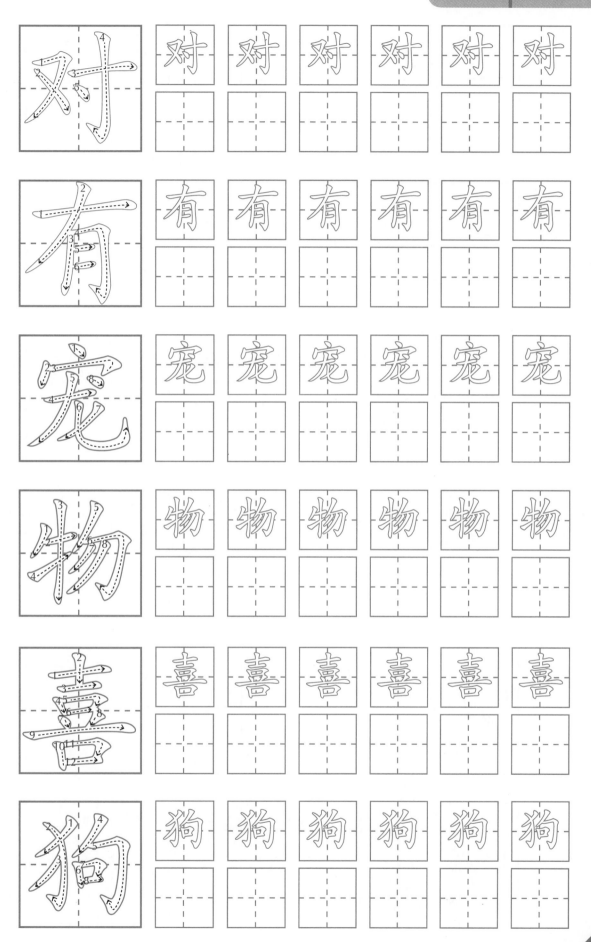

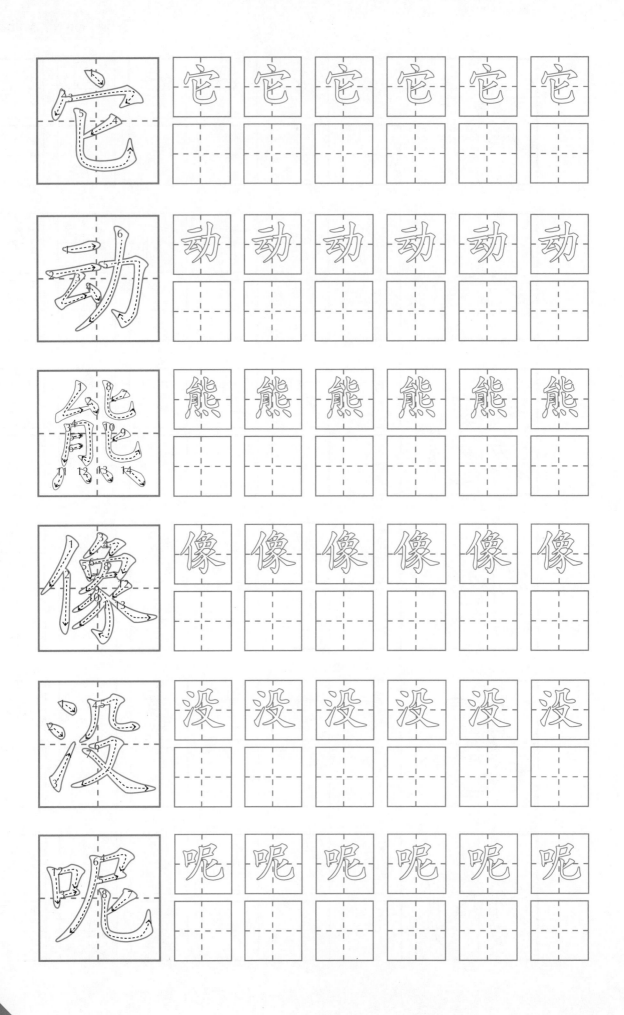

它 它 它 它 它 它

动 动 动 动 动 动

熊 熊 熊 熊 熊 熊

像 像 像 像 像 像

没 没 没 没 没 没

呢 呢 呢 呢 呢 呢

Have a try 试一试

① Look at the pictures and make conversations with
   your partner.
   看图说话

例：_____很高/胖/酷/漂亮。
   _____不高/胖/漂亮。

姐姐

爸爸

哥哥

叔叔

② Put the jigsaw pieces in the right position.
   选择正确位置

1. 妈妈 A 我 B 都很 C 喜欢 D 熊猫。
   和

2. A 你的 B 房间 C 漂亮 D 啊！
   好

3. A 他们 B 是 C 高中生 D 。
   都

③ On your own.
活动

Good friends 好朋友

Work in groups. Talk with each other about your good friends. Then put the information about them in the following form, including names, ages, appearances, favorite colors and favorite animals.

几人一组，互相介绍好朋友的名字、年龄、外貌、喜欢的颜色和喜欢的动物，并把其他同学说的话记在下面的表格内。

姓名	年龄	外貌	颜色	动物
玛丽	15	漂亮	白色	猫

Practice and learn 练一练

一 *Pinyin* exercises
拼音练习

① Listen to the CD and repeat.
听录音，并跟读下列音节

1. dang   deng   ding   dong
   tang   teng   ting   tong
   nang   neng   ning   nong
   lang   leng   ling   long

2. dāng   dēng   dīng   dōng
   tāng   téng   tǐng   tóng
   náng   néng   níng   nòng
   láng   lěng   lìng   lóng

② **Listen to the CD and then fill in the initials.**
听录音，填写声母

- **Please fill in the initials.**
  请填写声母

__ īng	__ áng	__ ōng	__ áng	__ ìng	__ èng
__ āng	__ ǒng	__ āng	__ ìng	__ óng	__ íng
__ ōng	__ ǐng	__ óng	__ éng	__ éng	__ āng
__ àng	__ ěng				

③ **Listen to the CD and then mark the tones.**
听录音，标出声调

1. qian   2. kuai   3. tian   4. gong   5. bo
6. zhong   7. xu   8. ye   9. qiong   10. nüe

④ **Listen to the CD and then circle the syllables you've heard.**
听录音，在听到的拼音上画圈

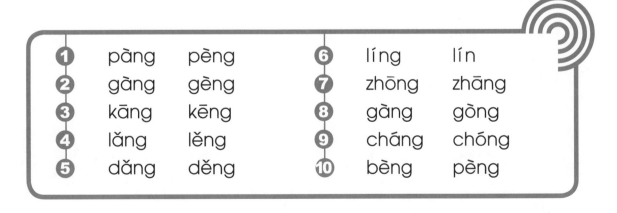

❶	pàng	pèng	❻	líng	lín
❷	gàng	gèng	❼	zhōng	zhāng
❸	kāng	kēng	❽	gàng	gòng
❹	lǎng	lěng	❾	cháng	chóng
❺	dǎng	děng	❿	bèng	pèng

二 Word exercises
词汇练习
① Matching.
连线

② Crossword puzzles.
填字游戏

Put the following words in the blanks.
请把下列汉字填在田字格里。

大中高学胖酷

真

生

三 Chinese character exercises
汉字练习
① Learn to recognize.
认汉字

Count the strokes of the following characters, and then compare your answers with your partner's.
数一数下列每个汉字有多少笔画，并与同伴比较一下，看谁数得对。

美　国　高　篮　球

② **Learn to divide.**
拆汉字

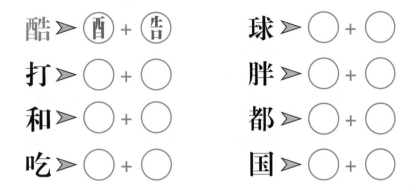

酷 ➤ ⟨酉⟩ + ⟨告⟩   球 ➤ ◯ + ◯

打 ➤ ◯ + ◯   胖 ➤ ◯ + ◯

和 ➤ ◯ + ◯   都 ➤ ◯ + ◯

吃 ➤ ◯ + ◯   国 ➤ ◯ + ◯

③ **Learn to write.**
写汉字

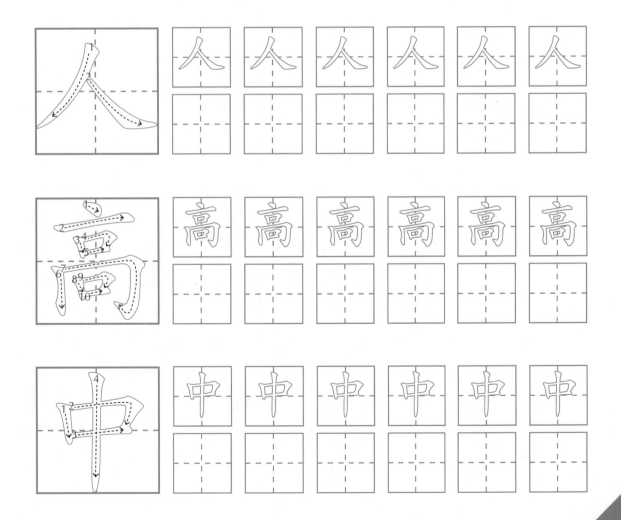

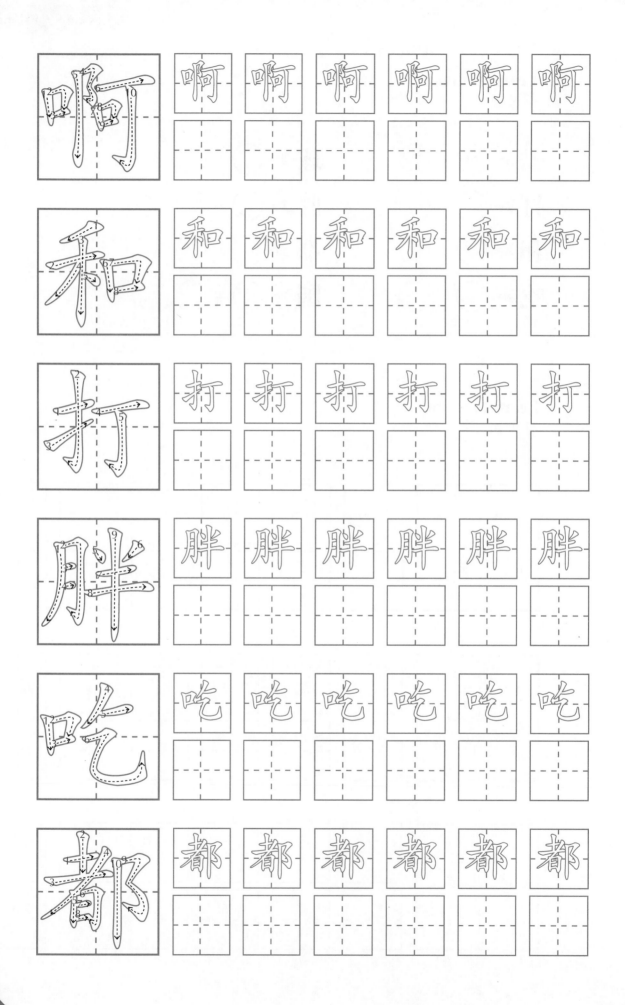

啊　啊　啊　啊　啊　啊

和　和　和　和　和　和

打　打　打　打　打　打

胖　胖　胖　胖　胖　胖

吃　吃　吃　吃　吃　吃

都　都　都　都　都　都

Have a try 试一试

① **Look at the pictures and make conversations with your partner.**
看图说话

例：他/她很_____，也很_____。
他/她喜欢_____，也喜欢_____。

她

猫

狗

高帅

他

篮球

零食

年轻　漂亮

② **Put the jigsaw pieces in the right position.**
选择正确位置

1. 美国 **A** 的 **B** 白宫 **C** 漂亮 **D** 。
   非常

2. **A** 妈妈 **B** 喜欢 **C** 电影 **D** 。
   看

3. 妹妹 **A** 喜欢 **B** 电影，**C** 喜欢 **D** 篮球。
   还

③ **On your own.**
活动

Celebrities 名人

Introduce one of your favorite celebrities, and tell others why you like him/her.
向大家介绍你喜欢的一位名人，并说说为什么喜欢他/她。

例：我喜欢的名人是_____，他(她)很_____。

Practice and learn 练一练

一 *Pinyin* exercises
拼音练习

① **Listen to the CD and repeat.**
听录音，并跟读下列音节

1.	gun	hun	lun		2.	dūn	tūn	lūn
	zhun	chun	shun			gǔn	hǔn	chǔn
	zun	cun	sun			jūn	qún	xún
	jun	qun	xun			zūn	cūn	sūn

② **Listen to the CD and then fill in the finals.**
听录音，填写韵母

• **Please fill in the finals.**
请填写韵母

d___ q___ c ___   z ___ ch ___ sh ___

k ___ r ___ s ___   x ___ t ___ g ___

j ___ h ___ zh ___

③ **Listen to the CD and then mark the tones.**
听录音，标出声调

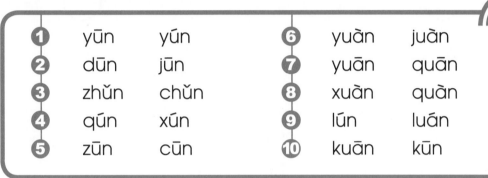

1. qun	2. niu	3. yun	4. lü	5. yin
6. shang	7. qi	8. guan	9. cong	10. ren

④ **Listen to the CD and then circle the syllables you've heard.**
听录音，在听到的拼音上画圈

❶	yūn	yún	❻	yuàn	juàn
❷	dūn	jūn	❼	yuān	quān
❸	zhǔn	chǔn	❽	xuàn	quàn
❹	qún	xún	❾	lún	luán
❺	zūn	cūn	❿	kuān	kūn

二 **Word exercises**
词汇练习

① **Matching.**
连线

影 帅 棒 白 宫 伟 知 著 演 员

shuāi
gōng
zhī
zhù
yuán
bàng
bái
wěi
yǐng
yǎn

② **Crossword puzzles.**
填字游戏

○ **Put the following words in the blanks.**
请把下列汉字填在田字格里。

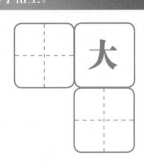

家
字
著
伟

大

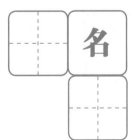

名

三 Chinese character exercises
汉字练习

① Learn to recognize.
认汉字

> Count the strokes of the following characters, and then compare your answers with your partner's.
> 数一数下列每个汉字有多少笔画，并与同伴比较一下，看谁数得对。

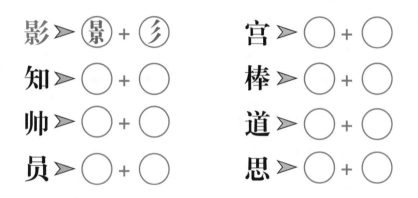

看〇 电〇 宫〇 非〇 员〇

② Learn to divide.
拆汉字

影 ➤ 景 + 彡   宫 ➤ 〇 + 〇

知 ➤ 〇 + 〇   棒 ➤ 〇 + 〇

帅 ➤ 〇 + 〇   道 ➤ 〇 + 〇

员 ➤ 〇 + 〇   思 ➤ 〇 + 〇

③ Learn to write.
写汉字

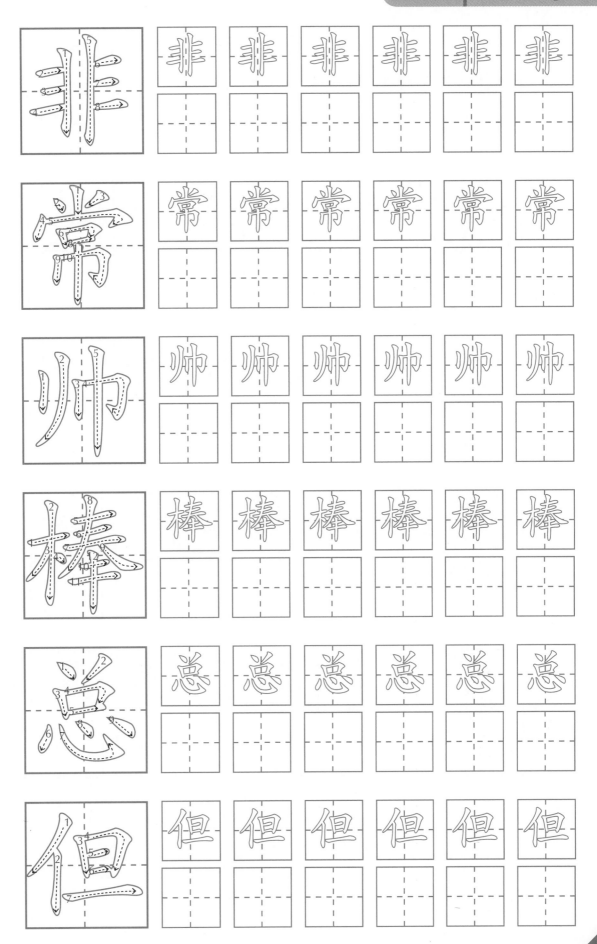

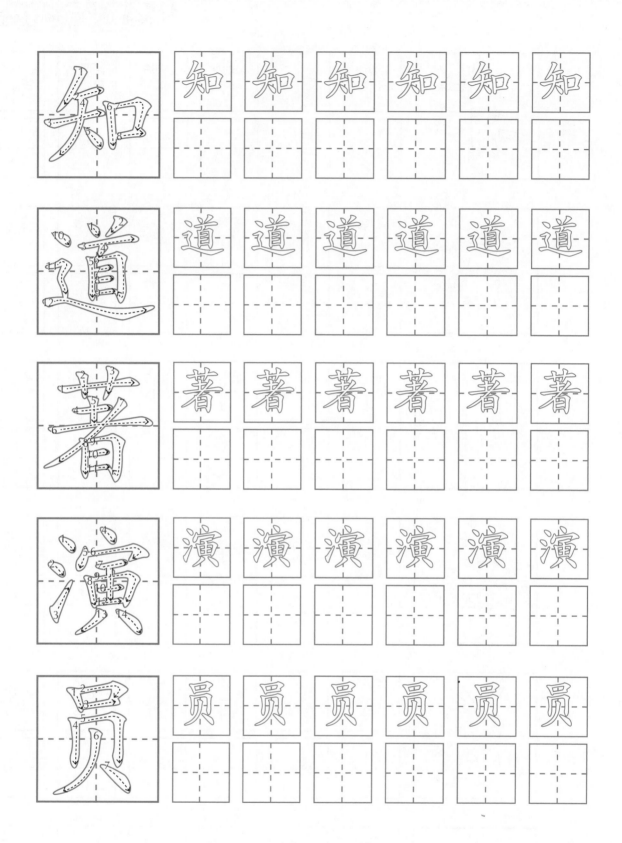

郑 重 声 明

图书在版编目（CIP）数据

体验汉语高中练习册. 第 1 册 / 国际语言研究与发展
中心. —北京：高等教育出版社，2008.6
ISBN 978-7-04-022260-9

Ⅰ.体⋯　Ⅱ.国⋯　Ⅲ.汉语－对外汉语教学－习题
Ⅳ.H195.4

中国版本图书馆 CIP 数据核字（2008）第 075024 号

策划编辑　徐群森　　**责任编辑**　金飞飞　　**责任印制**　朱学忠

出版发行	高等教育出版社	购书热线	010－58581350
社　　址	北京市西城区德外大街 4 号	免费咨询	800－810－0598
邮政编码	100120	网　　址	http://www.chinesexp.com.cn
总　　机	010－58581000		http://www.hep.com.cn
		网上订购	http://www.chinesexp.com.cn
经　　销	蓝色畅想图书发行有限公司		http://www.landraco.com
印　　刷	北京佳信达艺术印刷有限公司	畅想教育	http://www.widedu.com
开　　本	889×1194　1/16		
印　　张	4	版　　次	2008 年 6 月第 1 版
字　　数	113 000	印　　次	2008 年 6 月第 1 次印刷

本书如有印装等质量问题，请到所购图书销售部门调换。　　ISBN 978-7-04-022260-9